George Herriman, in an undated photo distributed by the International Film Service, New York. Would you play cards with this man?

KRAZY & IGNATZ.

by George Herriman.

"There is a Heppy Land, Fur, Fur Awa-a-ay - "

Comprising the Complete Full-Page Comic Strips,

1925-26.

Edited by Bill Blackbeard.

Fantagraphics Books, SEATTLE.

Published by Fantagraphics Books.
7563 Lake City Way North East,
Seattle, Washington, 98115, United States of America.

Edited by Bill Blackbeard.
Except where noted, all research materials appear courtesy of the San Francisco Academy of Cartoon Art.
Design and Decoration by Chris Ware.
Scans by Paul Baresh.
Promoted by Eric Reynolds.
Published by Gary Groth and Kim Thompson.

First Fantagraphics Books edition: March 2002.
Second edition: September 2002.
Third edition: December 2004.

ISBN 1-56097-386-2.

Printed in Korea.

  KRAZY & IGNATZ.

BY GEORGE, IT'S KRAZY!

Introduction by Bill Blackbeard.

Here it is — a bountiful new collection of one of the greatest works of American comic genius: two full years of George Herriman's inimitable classic comic work, a creation fit to rank with the cinematic work of Charlie Chaplin and W. C. Fields or the prose of Mark Twain and Bill Faulkner, hailed as the most richly creative comic strip of all time — and there's a pretty good chance it won't turn a buck. *Krazy Kat,* you see, doesn't sell at all well. The academic world of literary scholars (which activates the university presses) can't get over the fact that *Krazy Kat* is a comic strip and therefore not really fit for critical acclamation or reprinting, while the general bookbuying public is baffled by the seemingly outré goings-on that are the warp and woof of the strip's brilliance. (A national readership that only buys well-hyped good books because they're well-hyped and puts them away on their living-room prestige bookshelves unread, while devouring all of the Spillane and Ludlum they can get, is not a public that is going to embrace subtlety and poetic prose in a format where they are used to relishing *Marmaduke* and *The Family Circus.* Only the blessed few who recognize and rejoice in genius wherever it is found — in this instance the lifelong aficionados of *Krazy Kat* — are going to gleefully raid the exchequer in order to buy this latest collection of the Coconino chronicles, the best thing they know they will find in bookstores this year. This happy band never, unfortunately, fills publishers' coffers with sufficient protitable coin when a new kat collection is at hand.

This is why, sad to say, that during the fifty five plus years after George Herriman's death, there have been only grudging nibbles by publishers at the vast, precious oeuvre called *Krazy Kat,* some fourteen reprint volumes in all, comprising less than a third of the original newsprint work. All of Faulkner and Twain are snug in the American Library volumes, all of Chaplin and Fields are on videotape and DVD, but the greater part of Herriman remains accessible only in a single newsprint collection at the San Francisco Academy of Comic Art. The world's bookshelves have so far only sampled the artist's major work. Admittedly it would be risky for any institution or publishing house to undertake republication in full of the remaining nineteen years of Sunday pages and the remaining thirty-five years of daily episodes without a Rockefeller-sized grant. As it is, we will have to be content with the occasional bounty of a volume such as this and the promise of additional, similar volumes to come over the next few years if a sufficiently sophisticated and dedicated public at last emerges to support the hazardous undertaking. We'd be krazy not to hope this will happen.

But why has a comic strip, so obviously delightful to at least one group of readers — and I say obviously since most of you have certainly been rejoicing in the Herriman pages for some time before turning to this introduction — why has so witty and raucous and poetic a strip turned away so many readers who were inveterate strip fans (reveling in bright, imaginative, accomplished strips such as *Gasoline Alley, Bringing Up Father* and E. C. Segar's *Popeye*)? The almost universal response has been that they cannot fathom the point of the strip or its characters. They claimed (and claim) that the theme of Ignatz hitting Krazy with a brick was tiresome and that they could not understand most of the jokes; worst of all, they saw nothing engaging (i.e., cute) about the characters, as should damned well be the case with a funny animal strip. They were alienated. And because of this they could get angry and write blistering letters to the feature editors of the newspapers concerned. Most of these seemingly nervy journals were titles in the national chain commandeered by William Randolph Hearst, the fierce young publisher who ardently admired *Krazy Kat,* and who had to constantly fight with his editors, who begged for permission to drop the irritating strip. They claimed that they received endless letters complaining about this mystifying comic, which they had difficulties in answering since they found it mystifying themselves. The letters went unanswered and Hearst's edict prevailed; the kat comic stayed in his papers over the decades. There were a fair number of readers who agreed with Hearst, of course; some well known and some living abroad who had clipped kats sent to them, such as Gertrude Stein, Ernest Hemingway, Pablo Picasso, Gilbert Seldes, H. L. Mencken, Edmond Wilson, e e cummings, T. S. Eliot, and similar perceptive individuals who immediately appreciated Herriman's vagrant genius and who bought and cherished and wrote and talked about the infrequent book collections of the strip, following its newsprint appearances when they could.

The sustaining wonder of *Krazy Kat* is that we are so far from exhausting it. We have read the two Alices and know there can be no more mirrors or rabbit holes; we have closed the playground gate on Pooh for good and realize that the wind in the willows can never breath fresh in our enchanted faces again. After the better part of a lifetime we have found that even Dickens can be exhausted and that the grand gallery of Gamps and Pecksniffs and Pickwicks holds no more fresh figures to stroll the London streets with us through fog and lamplight. Yet we are able to rejoice in the knowledge that there are thousands of *Krazy Kat* episodes remaining to be fetched from their bourne of well tended newsprint and brought to our eyes by the present publisher, sales permitting — this trove of wonder at least remains fresh with the promise of continued delights to come.

George Herriman, the only son of Greek immigrants in Louisiana, who later took up residence in Los Angeles in the 1880s, whetted his creative pen on decorative newspaper graphics for the old *Los Angeles Herald* in the mid-1890s, aimed for cartooning success with a series of strikingly surreal gag cartoons accepted by Hearst's *San Francisco Examiner* just after the turn of the century, sealed his secure berth with some of the Sunday comic papers of his time by deftly adapting his bizarre comic viewpoint to the newly popular format of the comic strip with a delectable series of strips, such as *Lariat Pete, Major Ozone's Fresh Air Crusade, Alexander* (his first cat strip), *Bud Smith, Rosie's Mama,* and other four-color delights in the early 1900s. Taken aboard by the Los Angeles Examiner as a sports and news cartoonist in 1906, the young Herriman persuaded the sports page editor to let him fill space on newsless days with a series of trial balloon comic strips, beginning with race track gags and developing into the regularly printed Baron Mooch, in which a raffish duck attendent on the Baron took note of a forlorn waif of a kat he deemed "krazy." (The "k" was representative of Herriman's habitually surreal take on everything in general.) The duck took over the sports page strip after a bit and clowned through his own roisterous strip yclept Gooseberry Sprigg, the Duck Duke. Hearst (who read all of his papers cover to cover) liked what he saw in the duck duke strip and bid Herriman haste to the Hearst papers' HQ in New York, where he would be garbed in full syndication sable with the introduction of a family strip to be called *The Dingbats.* Herriman was not the cartoonist to be content with a routine family gag strip; he speedily introduced a mys-terious ménage of roomers who moved in over the Dingbats' apartment house quarters and made the Dingbats' life hellish with tricks and taunts, further maddening the family by deftly keeping out of sight so that the Dingbats could not so much as lay eyes on them. A burning desire to find out exactly who the upstairs family were and what they were up to came to obsess the Dingbats, and their continually ill-fated attempts to get a look at the people behind the plaster-cracking goings-on upstairs, composed the strip's primary theme for years. Logically enough the strip was renamed *The Family Upstairs.*

Herriman, however, was not content with adding a mystery family aboveboard in his new Hearst strip; he noted the apartment mouse which had begun to torment the Dingbat kat (yes; our krazy transplanted from the defunct Mooch epic) in pursuits under ad about the feet of the Dingbats, and moved the scrappy animal duo into a lower space of their own, which ran in tandem with the main Dingbat strip for several ensuing years. Here, in boisterous uproar and wit, began the classic strife between kat and mouse that was to evolve into the separate daily and Sunday *Krazy Kat* to come — and to endure so triumphantly through the funny page decades to come.

Yours in Herriman,
Bum Bill B.

MURPHY BELIEVES HE HAS CRACK PITCHER IN YOUNG FRED TONEY

CHICAGO AMERICAN SPORTS

TWENTY ROUND BOUTS LONG ENOUGH; BOXERS CAN DECIDE QUESTION

The Family Upstairs---Dingbat Is Completely Carried Away by Their Pet Stork---By Herriman.

The Family Upstairs, November 16th, 1910.

Dear Dook:

   Well, here's the "old man's" picture. Any fella with a face like that should keep it a secret from the public, and I can't see how you're going to get any circulation publishing mushes like that!

   Once, when a youth, I aspired to become a baker, a kneader of dough, to mould bread and fashion a doughnut or stencil a cookie. Full of the spirit of adolescence I buried a dead mouse in a loaf of bread once - it found its way into a tough family and not only did I get a sweet trimming but I got the air also. In another bakeshop, I thought it cute to salt the doughnuts instead of the accustomed sugaring. Wam!! "Stars" and everything - out on the pavement again - a good baker at large. Another shop; and I slit a 200 pound sack of flour over a four foot five inch baker - we barely got him out alive, when we did, looking like a "pose plastique", he took away the last remnant of ambition out of me.

   Then I became a cartoonist - as a sort of revenge on the world. We're doing our stuff for Mr. W. R. Hearst, but don't let him know anything about it. Oy, if he should know! And if you want to know it, we love the Desert - the dry (notice Dook, not a Chicago Desert, dry) old Desert, and that's where you will find us - when the last drop of ink is out of our bottle and the pen snaps.

                                   Yern,
                                   GEO HERRIMAN

8.

"The Gold Rush" as Seen by KRAZY KAT

By GEORGE HERRIMAN

(Mr. Herriman, the famous creator of the internationally famous comic supplement characters, Krazy Kat and Ignatz Mouse, has written this "krypticism" of Charlie Chaplin and "The Gold Rush" exclusively for THE CLASSIC.)

SO it's Komical Komments on "The Gold Rush," you wish I should make, eh, Mr. Editor, just that, and nothing more, heh?

That's a nice business you want me to engage in, Mr. Editor. I don't mind telling you that it's going to be a fine failure, yes sir, Mr. Editor, and about as useless as that extra R in fish.

Me, make kritical remarks, me analyze, me krack wise animadversions about holy shux, I should be so loose with my language, I should be so kareless with khirography, I should get so free with fustian. There be them, Mr. Editor, who make it a business to be kritics, dramatic kritics, that's a fine business, and there's a heap of dramatics in the world to get kritical about—there's dramatics on the stage even, and it's beginning to sprout among the movement pictures.

The opening khorus in "The Gold Rush" is very, very dramatic—in fact, it is "The Gold Rush"—men milling in the snow, hurling themselves into the white maw of the Arctic—fleas scampering across a klean sheet—you just know it's dramatics. So is a line of ducks flying from the pole to the pampas to lay an egg, or a ribbon of ants krossing the sidewalk to dissect a roach's kadaver, a Bowery bread line on Xmas Eve, a world's parade of airplanes, nose to tail, girdling the earth.

But about that Gold Rush, was it a thousand men, or a million—with their frozen sweat about them, panting up the Khilkoot—there was ages of snow beneath them, and the skies were ready to hurl ages more of it

upon them—yet the writhing string moved on, squirming its way into the open jaws of the North to pry from its white fangs a bit of its yellow fillings.

A large healthy, meaty bone upon which to do some kritical gnawing, Mr. Editor. But, out it faded, like a veil dissolving—and the march of a million men was something that had transpired eons ago—and on the echo of the last man's foot beats, the magic of transmutation takes place—from the musty metal in the krucible—arises enchantment—witchery in large flat shoes, baggy britches, swishing a reed, a billycock hat doffed to the universe, a gracious salutation, and the world acknowledges it with the smile of a child.

Charles Chaplin

There is no question of why he is here, slipping, sliding or scampering over the ice, no talk of the danger all about, depths below, heights above, bears behind, and ice all about—and we following, following, ever following. We have waited long to katch this sprite at play, so let no one stay our step while we have him—we will follow—whither he wills until he loses us in the mists and we flounder back to earth again. Rich man, poor man, beggar man, thief—leveled to a kommon denomination.

Why say that he made us laugh? Why say he made us cry? Why boast of his braveries?

A knight in armor on a horse aglitter with regal trappings never went into the fray for the love of his lady, or the advancement of chivalry with lighter heart than he. No social lion ever graced a banquet hall with more inspiring gentility—no friend ever stood by a pal with more self-sacrifice. No elf made more mischief—and, kould any maker of dreams have better awakened into the souls of a brace of buns stuck on the end of a pair of forks.

With apologies to the International Features Service

(Continued on page 80)

Herriman was at the height of his twenties vogue when the editor of *Movie Classics Magazine* (with *Photoplay* one of the two top selling movie mags of the time) had the nifty idea of asking him to seat Krazy in front of a projected print of a major feature of 1925 called *The Gold Rush* and transcribe his komments. They appeared as presented here in the October, 1925 issue, probably inducing much appreciative merriment in the hapless cinema kat named Charlie Chaplin, who wrote, directed, and starred in *The Gold Rush*. (The article, which was jumped in the original publication, finishes up here in a modern "resetting.")

the dance of a Pavlowa. What chef kould have brewed a stew from a shoe, from which would arise such gastronomic ecstasy — and what more perfect host than he — the white meat giving to his "guest," with the grand gesture. No favorite kourtier of a Stuart, or a Bourban, kould have been more graciously served — and all this in a desolate kabin in the Klondike.

A king of Babylon conjuring a royal fete for his queen kould not have more bravely battled the bitter bite of disappointment of finding her seat empty at the feast.

What Midas better born to his wealth.

Let all the kobblers of earth fashion flat shoes, all awry — and all the tailors trim trousers as loose as gunny sacks, put all the reeds of the world into kanes, and let the hatter go mad making Derbies — then pour into them the genius of another Chaplin.

It is as easy as writing kriticism — mes amis —

Twice as easy!!!!

And now, Ignatz!! The BRICK!!!

Left: The Herriman letter and art seen above appeared in the April, 1926 issue of *Ziff's*, a risqué digest-size cartoon and gag mag published by a young William B. Ziff, later co-founder of the Ziff-Davis publishing house, once noted for its giant size pulp magazines (*Amazing Stories*, etc.), and today a giant-sized investment firm. "Badzib" and "Duke" appear to be nicknames for Ziff, who apparently asked Herriman for some bio data and received what seems to have been a preprinted response sent by the cartoonist to most who wrote him. The balloon lettering doesn't appear to be Herriman's and was probably added by "Duke" Ziff to some stock drawings sent with the routine reply form. The regular "readers" of the raunchy Ziff's must have been startled at this odd intrusion of comic page denizens amid all the naughty Parisienne frou-frou they were used to.

KRAZY KAT SEES MISS DAVIES IN 'JANICE MEREDITH'

Cosmopolitan's New Picture "Janice Meredith" is Coming to the Strand Theatre Saturday.

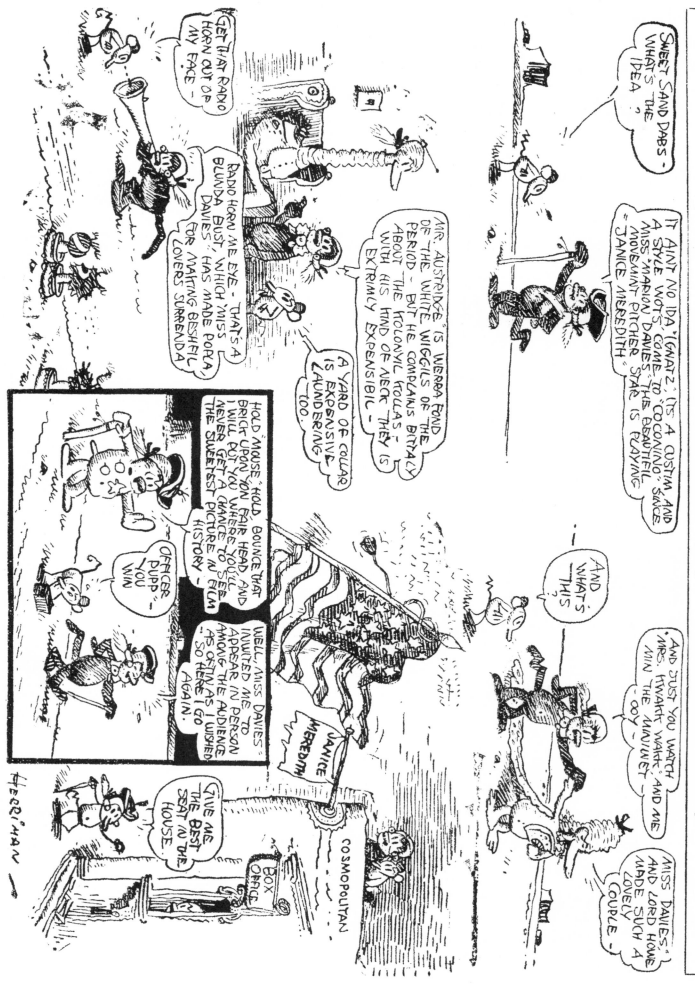

10.

Left: Herriman went bravely to bat in this gorgeous picto-review of Marion Davies' 1925 film from W. R. Hearst's Cosmopolitan Studios, a costume epic called *Janice Meredith.* One of a series of Hearst cartoonist reviews of Davies films in the 1920s (others were penned by Cliff Sterrett, Russ Westover, Jimmy Swinnerton, E. C. Segar, etc.), this elaborate charade printed in the *Seattle Post-Intelligencer* reflects Garge's keen desire to please the boss (which he knew would not be much of a problem) and, presumably, La Davies herself (which might have been less certain, in view of her later insistence that WRH force Segar to cut down on Popeye's "brutaliky" in the 1930s' *Thimble Theatre*). The P-I's own twaddle about the wonders of the Davies flick appeared below the Herriman spread. Unhappily, despite Officer Pupp's bold claim (obviously uttered with tongue firmly in cheek), the picture was not a notable hit with the critics of the non-Hearst press.

Above: An actual-size reproduction of one of Herriman's late-1920s *Embarrassing Moments* panel cartoons, showing the scale at which he worked, and the aggressive, confident pen line he brandished. Note that Herriman blacked in the right man's coat, as the checkered pattern with which he initially drew it wouldn't anchor the drawing as effectively as would a simple, bold shape. This drawing shows little, if any, evidence of pencilling, as well as demonstrating his characteristic knifework, at the leftmost edge of the tall man's face.

1925.

January 4th, 1925.

January 11th, 1925.

January 18th, 1925.

January 25th, 1925.

February 1st, 1925.

February 8th, 1925.

February 15th, 1925.

February 22nd, 1925.

March 1st, 1925.

March 8th, 1925.

March 15th, 1925.

March 22nd, 1925.

March 29th, 1925.

April 5th, 1925.

April 12th, 1925.

April 19th, 1925.

April 26th, 1925.

May 3rd, 1925.

KRAZY KAT   By HERRIMAN

May 17th, 1925.

May 24th, 1925.

May 31st, 1925.

Krazy Kat   By Herriman

June 7th, 1925.

June 14th, 1925.

_____

June 21st, 1925.

June 28th, 1925.

Krazy Kat

July 5th, 1925.

July 12th, 1925.

July 19th, 1925.

July 26th, 1925.

August 2nd, 1925.

August 9th, 1925.

August 16th, 1925.

August 23rd, 1925.

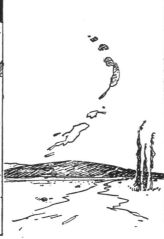

August 30th, 1925.

KRAZY KAT *by Herriman*

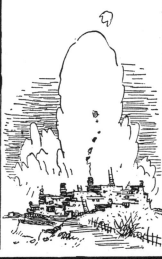

September 6th, 1925.

September 13th, 1925.

September 20th, 1925.

KRAZY KAT by Herriman

September 27th, 1925.

October 4th, 1925.

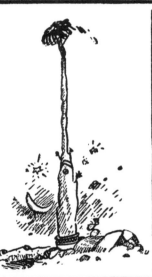

October 11th, 1925.

Krazy Kat   By Herriman

October 18th, 1925.

Krazy Kat

By Herriman

October 25th, 1925.

Krazy Kat

November 1st, 1925.

56.

Krazy Kat   By Herriman

November 8th, 1925.

November 15th, 1925.

November 22nd, 1925.

November 29th, 1925.

December 6th, 1925.

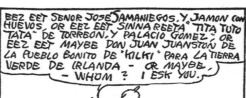

December 13th, 1925.

Krazy Kat   By Herriman

December 20th, 1925.

December 27th, 1925.

1926.

Krazy Kat

January 3rd, 1926.

Krazy Kat

By Herriman

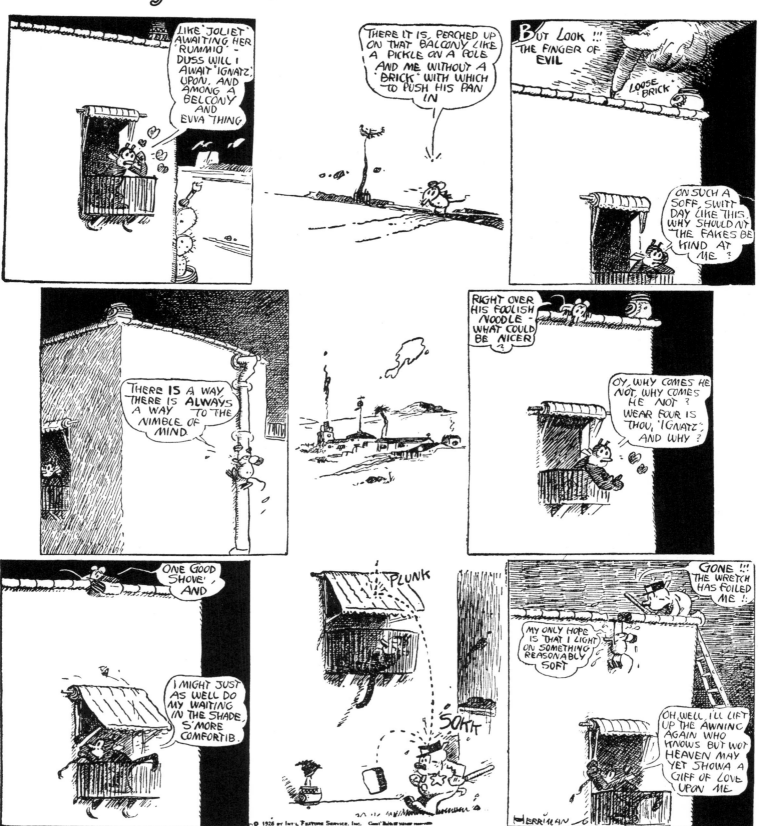

January 10th, 1926.

Krazy Kat

January 17th, 1926.

January 24th, 1926.

January 31st, 1926.

February 7th, 1926.

February 14th, 1926.

February 21st, 1926.

February 28th, 1926.

Krazy Kat

By Herriman

March 7th, 1926.

March 14th, 1926.

March 21st, 1926.

March 28th, 1926.

April 4th, 1926.

April 11th, 1926.

April 18th, 1926.

April 25th, 1926.

Krazy Kat

By Herriman

May 2nd, 1926.

May 9th, 1926.

May 16th, 1926.

May 23rd, 1926.

May 30th, 1926.

June 6th, 1926.

June 13th, 1926.

June 20th, 1926.

June 27th, 1926.

July 4th, 1926.

July 11th, 1926.

July 18th, 1926.

KRAZY KAT

The aromatic fragrance of a 'brick' a'bake smites 'Ignatz Mouse's tremulous nose, and suffuses his soul with a glistering glow of glory

Like Steel to the Magnet.

Fate deals him a kind hand — the guerdon of his quest is full of an unctuous, & oleaginous amplitude of gratification

July 25th, 1926.

Krazy Kat

August 1st, 1926.

Krazy Kat

By Herriman

August 8th, 1926.

Krazy Kat

August 15th, 1926.

Krazy Kat

By Herriman

August 22nd, 1926.

August 29th, 1926.

September 5th, 1926.

September 12th, 1926.

Krazy Kat

By Herriman

September 19th, 1926.

KRAZY KAT ∴ By Herriman

September 26th, 1926.

October 3rd, 1926.

October 10th, 1926.

October 17th, 1926.

Krazy Kat

By Herriman

October 24th, 1926.

Krazy Kat

By Herriman

October 31st, 1926.

November 7th, 1926.

November 14th, 1926.

November 21st, 1926.

November 28th, 1926.

December 5th, 1926.

December 12th, 1926.

December 19th, 1926.

December 26th, 1926.

The IGNATZ MOUSE DEBAFFLER PAGE

for 1925-1926.

1/4/25: "kayceebee" This seemingly cryptic reference was understood on sight by 1925 readers; "KCB" was the byline of a widely read Hearst columnist who composed his rather twee daily commentaries on the esteemed Allen Sundry in fragmented comic verse made up of a half dozen words or so per line.

2/22/25: "Oy, wam-pie!!!" Krazy is accusing the inkomplete kat of seducing Ignatz, calling the creature a "vampire," which was 1920s slang for a female seductress, often shortened to plain "vamp." The notorious screen star, Theda Bara (Arab Death with letter juggling), was one such. Krazy's outraged "wam-pie" holds a curious nomenclatural hint of a great comic character to emerge, hamburger hungry, from the enchanted pen of Elzie Crisler Segar a few years later.

3/8/25: "Private stock" All of the frenetic goings-on in this majestic episode will be grasped at once if it is recalled that in 1926 prohibition ruled. Later on, as you will discover to your delight, Joe Stork is corrupted by the temptations of the social scene into becoming a bootlegger, bearing bottles rather than babes.

8/8/25: "Seldesian" Herriman here speaks of a distinguished "patron of art" named Gilbert Seldes, who first celebrated the wonders of the Coconino crew in his 1922 best seller, *The Seven Lively Arts,* which was the first considerable work to dare suggest that the comic strip might actually be a new art form. (Shh! The notion is still scandalous!)

8/16/25: What's that potted tree in the middle of Offisa Pupp's harangue on the nobility of the brick? A glance at the following pages will display more apparently irrelevant vignettes at stage center, all the way to the end. The party responsible was not, of course, Herriman, but none other than his chief mentor and champion among national journalists, W. R. Hearst, who wanted more public appreciation of the wondrous witchery wrought weekly by Herriman's brick ballet. Hearst was only too sadly aware of the aversion felt by the broad newspaper public toward the strip, and in 1925 thought he had hit on a possible

solution – to hit his own enormous readership between the eyes – zip, pow! – with a brickbat spread of the strip across the first two inside Saturday pages of his largest circulation paper, the New York Evening Journal. To make the impact WRH wanted, only eight panels, all greatly enlarged from those normally found in the tabloid format strip, were needed – four across the bottom of each page. The effect was grand. But the other Hearst papers, with their individual editors, wanted no part of this comic strip apotheosis in their journals; they had been happy with the tabloid layout they had been running. The reassembly of the eight large panels Herriman was now drawing into the tab format, however, left a huge hole in the middle – which Herriman, with characteristic felicity, filled with a weekly vignette unrelated to the Coconino danse Micawber that encircled it.

9/20/25: "Kokonino" In spite of Herriman's propensity for subbing hearty "k's" for nomenclatural "c's" throughout his kat work, he generally left the name of its locale, an actual Coconino County in Arizona, unaltered. This usage is a rare exception.

1/17/26: Herriman greatly relished spending his idle hours away from Higgins and Strathmore at the nearby Keystone Studio where his slapstick buddies rollicked through a couple of two reelers a week to his enormous pleasure and edification. Some of this input emerges in this highly cinematic episode, to the delectation of all except Ignatz, who might have done better to disguise his brick in a Keystone-ready custard pie, which neither rain nor Kop could have kept from collision with Krazy's cabeza on *that* set.